Becoming an Island

Becoming an Island

Copyright © 2021 by Anthony Febo

ISBN: 978-1-7358864-1-1

All rights reserved. No portion of this book may be reproduced in any form without permission from the publisher, except as permitted by U.S. copyright law.

Cover design by Mar Spragge.

Cover layout by Mar Spragge.

http://www.marspragge.com/

Edited by Story Boyle, Liv Mammone, and Josh Savory.

Formatted by Josh Savory.

Game Over Books
www.gameoverbooks.com

I.

8   tonight i'm cooking

10   lifelong dance partners

12   showering as a form of healing

14   tostones: a how-to guide

16   bendicion pai

18   grown from

21   wisdom to know the difference

23   i said she said

26   hipocrita

28   until then

30   salsa

33   arriving in two parts

35   excerpt from my vows

II.

39   when i lost my first taekwondo tournament at 17 years old

41   my father's heart is less like a bloody knuckle after a bar fight and more like the stitches used to heal the wound

43   far, far away

45   my father is a country boy   i am city kid

46   truth is

48   side eye while i uber drive volume 3

49   side eye while i uber drive volume 4

51   first time

53   i wonder what ricky martin is doing right now

55   poem in the voice of the cat i stayed with for 10 days

58   lobo domesticado

60   men in my family

62   6/17/18

63   shadows

66   good morning

70   acknowledgements

72   biography

I.

No one tells you how alone writing can feel. Coming from the stage where the voice carries intention, where movement tells a story, where eyes watch and accept their own translations. Writing, where the words alone are the art is the most vulnerable I've felt since the first time I got booed offstage in seventh grade. I've tightened my grip around these poems while making this book. I've landlocked these poems around myself. Comfort made me forget what lies beyond my reach. I've gotten so used to highways that I forgot about ports, about airplanes. I'm still keeping these poems close to my chest but now I'm expanding my own body. *Becoming an Island* is more of a declaration than a title, more of an identity than a job. I breathe, and I feel a finger loosen. I breathe, and tension in my forearm is gone. I breathe, and finally let go.

TONIGHT I'M COOKING

because I miss the creation my hands can make
too often I focus on my knuckles
and tonight I'd rather use the precision of my fingers to cut plantains
place them in a pan and watch them tan in oil
like if I never moved from Puerto Rico would my skin be tostones brown

how I cook to feel closer to home
how this has nothing to do with who can cook better
and everything to do with the man on the train that yelled

English, please!

when I was just giving directions to someone in Spanish
how he was trying to make space for his ignorance
by diminishing my culture
how there is no correct way to be Latino in public
after being told to

shut up

without proving that person right

so tonight
I need to cook
need to take something dead
massage it with Adobo
let it get loose to the song of oil and sweat
then watch it give life to those that eat it

tonight we will eat
tonight we will praise our food
  and not worry about the language we do it in
tonight the stereotype of being Latino and loud does not exist here

we are all too busy reteaching our mouths
  how to be a host for this food
how to leave room for dessert
because there is always dessert at my house
and they all have names
that don't have names in English
because when you taste this good there is no need for translation
there is no *english please* for flavor
for tradition that keeps culture alive
because we all need to eat
because we all need to live
because what's the point of doing either without a little Sazón
like the next motherfucker that yells

English please!

must be bitter
like they must be what they eat
like tonight
I will be
an island

LIFE LONG DANCE PARTNERS

so there I was
dancing at a houseparty in Roxbury
and everything in this moment was so. damn. lit.
the DJ
who was technically the homeowner
with a really good 90s Spotify playlist
was still the DJ
and I swear she was reading my mind
cause every song she played brought me and this girl closer
and *closer* ya'll
was the theme of the night

now this is not the first time her and I have moved
we've tap-danced with conversations that produced a melody
that made anyone listening to us be like
yea yea yea that sounds familiar
like something my parents used to play
and it's like we've been here before
like we were lifelong dance partners
like this moment can transcend time

I am 12 years old
and all I know about rhythm
is that it tastes like my first kiss on a rooftop in Puerto Rico
while downstairs
at my sister's 6-year-old birthday party
there is waaaayyy too much reggaeton being played

I am 14
at my first high school gathering
and literally the two step is saving my life
until this girl with moon-like hands
guides the blood in my hips to move with hers

I am 21
and all that practicing with my long sleeve tee shirts
in front of my mirror is paying off
this dance floor is mine
Sean Paul is egging me on
and I am dutty wining straight into the heart of a girl

I once thought was too good for me
I am here
in this moment
dancing with her in a Roxbury apartment
my feet
tiptoeing around the fact that I like her
my hips
howling and thankful for this moon
my forehead
dedicated to keeping in theme with the night

she is close
and ya'll this is not the first time her and I have moved
but it's the first time we've touched
and it's innocent
it's pure
it's an achievement to my bones
it is a moment I don't know if I'll ever get to share with her again
so I take a step back and look at her
with just enough grin for her to know that when the clouds are out
stretching themselves across the sky waiting to twirl with the stars

that's when I'll think of her
how every night
holds the potential
for anyone
to have a moment
like this

SHOWERING AS A FORM OF HEALING

I think it's fucked up
that waking up and hating myself a little bit less than yesterday
is considered a victory
but I will celebrate nonetheless
I will eat just enough candy as a reward
before it becomes another reason to chastise myself
I will drink just enough rum to feel the warmth in my hands
instead of drinking to forget the cold that engulfs me

I still hate myself
but at least today I wore different clothes
I took a shower
not as an excuse to cry but as an actual form of self-love
didn't even use soap
didn't need to
it's my third shower of the day

and today
I saw myself naked
and the mirror didn't mock me for the elasticity of skin
I saw myself naked
and the lack of clothing didn't remind me
of the lack of love I sometimes have for myself
and dammit that is a reason for festivities

so I will play music
and sing as the water takes notice of the deficiency in my bones
how they require extra energy to move nowadays
how my marrow is devoid of sunlight
so for now this water will do
and I will cry to that
not because I'm sad
which I still am

but I'm crying because my body is still capable
of sprouting something beautiful
even in the midst of all this darkness
as neglect tries to make a desert of this body
and tomorrow I might hate myself still
even more than today
but right now
I am drenched
I am naked
I am okay

TOSTONES: A HOW-TO GUIDE

first make sure your knife is as sharp as the words that cut you
rinse it off with water and soap

note:
no amount of cleaning will make
filthy spic!
feel any less sharp

next pick up your green plantain
it should be thick in your palm
and be as green as the 71 billion dollar debt
the U.S. has placed Puerto Rico in

cut the edges
take joy in the sound the blade makes
when it is slammed against the board
this will make the blade duller
but you've wanted a new knife anyways

gut the plantain vertically down the middle
with your thumbs remove the green
and notice the plantain's eagerness to be creative and alive

now that it is free
it's time to support the plantain through its separation
make each slice know
that just because it isn't together anymore
doesn't mean it should feel any less whole
each slice should know
that it has the potential to exist as the single most delicious toston
that despite its prior captivity
now is its time to shine

so dress them in their best Adobo outfit
place them in the oil and let them sing

their song sounds like the free fall of that good love
the type of love that lets you know you will be full
the type of love that hurts if you move too fast too quick

so wait
allow the plantain to absorb the shine
until its blush becomes permanent
turn it over
make sure the other side gets love too
because even in freedom
it's necessary to be aware of the space that is taken

once it looks like it has been to the island that birthed it
take it out
have the tostonera hug it
the way an aunt does after years of not seeing you
the embrace should reveal the parts of the plantain that were too shy
to get dressed and dance
but no one has roots at this party that don't sway like palm trees

put them back in
this time the song sounds more like an encore than it does a final bow
when they are ready
have a paper towel on a plate waiting to soak up the sweat while you
prepare a bowl of Adobo, ketchup, and mayo for them to dive into
because what is better than a little dip after a night of celebration

note:
this recipe isn't for hunger
it's for healing
for carving out life when others condemn you for being more than salt
when parts of your existence are ingredients that others can't pronounce

so eat and be full
buen provecho my friends
buen provecho

BENDICION PAI

I write this knowing it will never be a part of you. If language is a barrier, then my Spanish, your English, are prison bars that keep us from ever truly being free to grasp what the other is saying.

te amo

I haven't always been able to say that.

no te entiendo
pero te acepto
y quiero que sepas que te adragesto las cosas que me has enseñado

When you were nine, and you first learned of life by watching your father die of Alzheimer's, did you decide to live more in the moment in fear that your memories would betray you? I am afraid I am a product of the reckless. That my decisions are founded in the knowledge that I too will forget my regrets and die with a false sense of a clear conscience. That I will forget the weight of burden and exist until the end of my days with buoyancy in my breath. But I don't want to be remembered that way. Papi, how do you want to be remembered? Papi, what do you want to remember?

papi tengo miedo que un dia me vas a olvidar
y se que no vas hacerlo a propósito
yo se que tu me quieres
que por me tu le mete la mano a cualquiera
que tu estas listo para enseñarle la mata vaca del barrio campo
así que papi
necesito que peles

I forgive you, dad. By which I mean I forgive myself for the hold I allowed you to have on me and call it your fault. My forgiveness does not come with an erasure of your actions. It comes with a processing of where they came from, and how that has affected me, and what I want to do about it.

And what I want to do about it is choose to love you; the man you are now which also includes the man you were then. Let's create a new language that will allow us to communicate what the moment needs in order for you to know that I love you.

papi a veces me consumo con la pesadilla
que ya me has olvidado
y me olvido que todavía tenemos tiempo
le doy tanto energía al miedo de perderte
que pierdo tiempo escuchándote reir

When I think back to the first time I saw you again after you left to Puerto Rico to start construction on our house, I don't remember the plane ride or the drive from the airport, I just remember understanding why you were the way you were. How at the core of your existence, you are someone who loves and someone that is loved.

If there is one thing I want to learn about home,
it's how to be someone like that.

entonces papi
camina conmigo
tengo algunas preguntas
no importa si sabes las respuestas
solo te quiero escuchar hablar

GROWN FROM

I was grown from arroz con gandules
from sofrito and adobo can fix any meal
from my house on Sundays looking like a Goya commercial

I was grown from music
from calling Willie Colón and Héctor Lavoe my godfathers
learning Spanish like
tu amor es un pedriódico de ayer
from calling Big Pun and Terror Squad my cousins
learning my own language like
dead in the middle of Little Italy
little did we know that we riddled two middlemen who didn't do diddly

I was grown from cobblestone streets
from hearing
I can't wait to leave this place
from knowing what it's like to run for my life
from having outsiders know more about my city than I did
from being surrounded by people who hate their own skin

I was grown from this skin
from not being dark enough to hang with the Ricans
from not being light enough to hang with the whites
from being confused about where to sit at lunch
from not knowing who had my back when I got into fights

I was grown from hers
from my mother bringing me into this life
from my best friend showing me what to do with my life
from my first love making me question my life
from my second love making me question my life
from my current love making me thankful for life
from being thankful

I was grown from being thankful
from knowing what love is from parents who love each other
from knowing what love is from parents who hate each other
from knowing that sometimes
that's what love is in a Spanish household
from having lived in the city and in the *campo*
from falling asleep to police sirens and to coquís
from experiencing all four seasons and summer all year round

yea I was grown from du-rags and Timbs
from buying XXL tee shirts and 40" waist jeans
  when I weighed 135 pounds
from not knowing where I fit in
from waking up every morning and wearing clothes that I did not fit in

I was grown from the pen
from listening to Mos Def and reading Shakespeare
  was just a common weekend
from losing my notebook in high school and swearing
  I would never write again

but I was grown from trying again
from my mother
being forced to drop out of school to watch over her siblings
then getting her GED
then getting her Bachelor's
then getting her Master's
then becoming a teacher
just so she can come home with enough time
  to tuck my sister and me into bed

from my father
being the youngest of twelve
watching his father die from Alzheimer's when he was nine
then watching six of his siblings do the same in the past five years
knowing it will happen to him
but waking up yesterday
running seven miles then going to work
and waking up today and doing the same thing again

see, I was grown from being proud
from wearing the red, white, and blue and one star on my chest
from having the Merrimack flow through my veins
from having Febo for a name

I was born with Febo as my name
and if I were to be born again
may I be born with everything the fucking same

WISDOM TO KNOW THE DIFFERENCE

there is a cottage in this chest
enough folks have come here in search of something sweet
and have left with parts of them missing
to know who the villain is
I do not pretend that this is a safe space
I do not know where the candy cane railings
or the gumdrop door knobs came from
but I haven't made any moves to tear them down

I am always hungry
always in search of what will keep me full
but it's not these trophies
I never wanted them mounted on my walls
they are here to remind me that my gluttony can kill

I sleep next to another forest
her chest is a community of trees
all the elements for living stacked in such a way
that it feels like they were formed in harmony
here the fire lights itself
here people visit and they walk away whole
here the owner calls herself a witch and the magic she conjures, she shares

what does it mean to be the holder of good?
the distributor of dreams?
when I cut down my first tree
I did it knowing that I was taking a home from someone
justified it by claiming that I too needed shelter
but we all need shelter
a place to lay our heads at night
who am I to lay mine next to someone so enchanted?
someone who loves like it's her first language
gives of herself like it's her love language

see my wife
made me an ax for our wedding night
told me that's as far as she will go the rest is up to me
there's a cottage in this chest made from replanted trees
the walls are filled with art that we made

we have dessert every night.

I SAID SHE SAID

I said
Carlie, do you trust me?
and she said
I trust you, Febo.
then fell back into my arms

later we told each other the first trust fall was the scariest
and that was the point
before we incorporated her falling off the table,
we wanted the first of the five to be a straight trust fall
we did five trust falls as a closing performance
to our first art show as our collective Make Art and Cry
        we did five trust falls for the five months we were not together

I asked
Carlie, do you trust me?
because it was I who broke it
I made trust a dirty word
so when she answers
it is not just for the performance
it is a reminder that forgiveness sometimes feels like falling

she said
I trust you, Febo.
and flung her body off the table
surrendering her limbs to gravity
the crowd gasping as her hair brushed the floor
her eyes opened to find me smiling back—
because at this point we both know that if she ever hits the bottom again
it won't be because I wasn't there to catch her

I said
Carlie, do you trust me?

and it is no longer a performance
it's an application
an interview for a position I am not worthy of but fuck do I want it
she said

I trust you, Febo.
and we are both flying—
not away from the mistakes I've made
but towards a deconstruction of my masculinity
towards a deconstruction of her privilege
and we are both showing up to do the work—

I said
Carlie, do you trust me?
and I think about all the lies I told her
I think about the crying when she found out
and the shame feels so heavy in my arms
she said
I trust you, Febo.
and I believe her
the same way I believed her when she said
I'm not asking you to make a choice but if you don't you will lose me
so I let go of shame and held on to her instead

and it's not that I can't live without her
I just don't want to
I mean why would I
we've proven that communication works
that unlearning patriarchy works
that creating the space to grow and challenge each other works

the last of the five was supposed to be another straight trust fall
the idea being

that doing this again after everything that had just happened should
make what once felt horrifying now feel like something we could
approach courageously

but this time
I got in front of her
humbled myself
asked her to take the biggest leap of faith

she said yes

we got married in June

HIPOCRITA

when my father learned how many of his sins were splintered in my feet
he sat me down and talked to me like I hadn't seen his horns
like I was unaware of the tsunamis that can be caused
by touching a body that isn't one you've called home
like I haven't fallen asleep to the concert of shattered glass
or counted my bruises instead of sheep
the night my lover discovered the real weight of my name

she whispered
I trusted you to be better than your father
and I've never felt anything with that much reverb

I sat there
on the broken futon in my parents basement
listening to my dad pretend that I am not his mirror
as if my father does not lead every interaction
with my younger cousins:
how many girlfriends do you have?

and I sat there
slowly turning into a riddle
wondering if my tongue still remembered the Spanish word for hypocrite
wondering how many headshots would it take for me
to kill my teenage self rising from the grave I buried him in
because that version of me hated my dad for the same reason
he is talking to me now

and I can't spell irony without capitalizing the *I*
how it was *I* that held the door open for lust
I said treat this like your home
don't worry about tracking in dirt
thought *I* could just sweep it under the rug
but *I* was unaware of how much my floors needed cleaning

now i am in my parents basement
being told I shouldn't treat women the way I do
by the man that taught me how to do it
and I guess that is growth
and I guess to love my father is to practice forgiveness
I learned that from the way my mother still laughs at my father's jokes
how my mother didn't laugh for the two years they were separated
how she hasn't laughed since I moved back to their basement
I guess I reminded her of the parts of my father she has forgiven

UNTIL THEN

I know the day will come when my father will not recognize me
or he will stare and wonder why this stranger has his eyes
or he will hear me make a joke
my attempt to make the room more human
everyone will laugh
he won't know why this feels familiar

or he'll remember me at the age he loved me the most
ask me how did I grow up so fast
I'll rebuild a smile
say it's in my genes
and won't make him feel guilty for forgetting
all the years I loved him back

or he will tell me stories about his son
the one that looks just like me
how he could have been a great martial artist
if he just would have stuck to it
and I swallow a thousand apologies in Spanish

he will lay in the comfort of his own bed
or in a hospital
or in a shelter
whatever my mom decides
either way it will not be home
but I will play El Gran Combo, Celia Cruz, Héctor Lavoe
his foot will begin to twitch
and I'll watch this small flicker of light
be enough for a house party in his skin

I know the day will come when my father will not recognize me
it is a version of myself I do not want to meet

until then
I laugh at the same old stories
share a beer with him in secret
keep reminding him that yes, I did get married
and take advantage of being able to call him
while he can still pick up and say

¡Hijo! ¿Como estas?

SALSA

if you are unfamiliar with the structure of salsa music
well it is simple

two verses
a chorus
and a bridge

but for those of us whose feet step in rhythm with timbales
we await the real reason to take the dance floor

the breakdown

the part where the song is technically over
but it would be sin for the musicians to stop
because when you sing salsa music you singing Spanish gospel
and tonight Marc Anthony is God

the opening trumpet asks if you've ever heard of Jesus
and before you can reply you hear him

mirándote a los ojos se responden mis porqués

and now all your *why God why's* are turned to WEPA
you laugh at all the times you felt sorry for yourself
 because you could have been dancing

me inspiro en tus palabras y mi casa está en tu piel

now your hands are free from the shackles
 of your pockets and they are looking for life ya'll
looking for a reason to believe that this shit will get better
at least for one song
as if all your heaviness can be shaken off with a spin

que tierno amor, mi devoción, viniste a ser mi religión

and there she is
the only dance partner that has ever mattered
she's known you since your two left feet would stumble just to say hello
and she is here gliding on the dance floor
and you are thirteen and in love all over again
but she is no fallen angel
so this must be Heaven
and if this is Heaven
then you are thankful for the fire that has burned you

mi dulce sentimiento, de nada me arrepiento

she tells you she is tired
that she's been doing the same moves for

two verses
a chorus
and a bridge
and she is ready to

break down

but you pull her close
and like a prayer you whisper
but the breakdown
is the part we've all been waiting for

valió la pena lo que era necesario para estar contigo amor

you tell her
that after hearing her laugh for the first time
you went home and searched through your father's Bible collection
  so you could finally understand what God was singing about
that if you ever get a chance to kiss her confession booth mouth
may all your sins be rebuked

may the seconds that it takes for your lips to touch
  be a final toast to the road that led to her

las horas y la vida a tu lado nena, están para vivirlas pero a tu manera

you reflect back on your two verses
your chorus
and your bridge
how so many times you have stopped moving

how that felt so unholy

cause now
your hearts are in sync with the rhythm of timbales
and you are thankful for this Gospel
thankful for speaking God's language
and thankful for the time it has taken for you
  to finally gather the courage to ask her to dance in this

church

enhorabuena. porque valió la pena, valió la pena

arriving in two parts

Outside

i step out of my door
and i greet myself in this setting with three breaths
one for who i was when i woke up
an ellipsis of the p.m. i surrendered to
i breathe
and choose today as a new page
stillness
caused by choosing to be still
is a stillness i can build on
the second breath is for who i want to be
a smile for a stranger
a *bless you* for a sneeze
no *thank you* required
i want to be a held door for ease of transitions and nothing else
here, i'm reminded why the tops of trees are called crowns
how empires are grown from legacy
how i am a manifestation of my parents sacrifice
the third breath is for me
now
in this moment
with gratitude in my back pocket and intention jingling in my hand
the me that is now three breaths deep
in my understanding of my own skin today
if i dont slow down enough to hear the echoes of my own body
begging me to be validated
how can i begin the healing process?
the tending of my own garden
the refurbishing of my own kitchen
like how can i buy new cabinets before i empty
measure
and rip out the cabinets that were there before

i carry this third breath with me in my stride
until it eventually transforms into the breath that wishes my wife
goodnight the breath that thanks her for saying yes everyday
the breath that carries the final *I love you* of the night
before i find a new one tomorrow morning

The Arboretum

and notice
how New England grants us the opportunity to learn from nature
how the seasons are different enough to have their own personalities
and if we let them
they can teach us about change
how to mourn and let go
how to celebrate rebirth
how to live in that fullness
how to prepare for the inevitable winter all over again
the poets are supposed to love nature
we are suppose to find the beauty of a leaf fall
are expected to make music out of the engraving of foot in snow
are known for engineering words to make the sun brighter
and i guess
i'm here for that
here to feel it first before i swallow the forest whole
need to chew it in my own mouth
need to feel my own toes grow numb while i search for a seat
that will frame my thoughts
need to forget what my body was like before this choice
each step i take
i plant batches of fresh soil in the parts of me once filled with shame
i meet myself where i'm at
put it in harmony with what is
and isn't this
so breathtaking?

excerpt of my vows

i did, i do, i will keep doing

1.

I'm often called a dreamer by realists unhappy
with their reality and a dreamer I had to be to find you
because my reality would have never let me accept
that a dream like you could be real
I vow to consider always how much you need sleep
to let you dream when I wake up hours earlier than you
because I know you let me dream when an idea forms
how you explore the corners of possibilities with me
encourage me to push through
and are somehow already on the other side
smiling
assuring me that this is how things will always be
a constant back-and-forth of support
a space to build off the other's suggestion
an open field every time we speak

2.

have you noticed
that when you wake up
we do this thing where we look at each other
and there's a pause
then a smile creeps up on our faces
it's like the light slowly revealing itself after a storm cloud passing
like this is where we fall in love all over again
and shit it's usually 7ish in the morning at that point
and isn't that how a day should start?
and doesn't that answer the question of my inspiration's origin?
and wouldn't you too want to spend the rest of your life
with a love like that?

3.

yes. I do. I will. I'm here. for you. always. you know it. affirmative on the love. Roger Roger on this choice. loud and clear about the commitment. you got it Jack. by which I mean Carlie. I mean lover. I mean friend. I mean most trusted confidant. the only person to truly see me. the only person I have truly seen. I got you. no worries. just breathe. what do you need? where does that come from? how does that make you feel? what do you want to do about it? yes you can lay here. yes we can walk. yes I can listen. yes, we can just hold this moment. yes. I do. I will. I'm here.

II.

I can't speak for other islands, but mine is warm. Mine has beaches that stretch as far as your dreams can take you. Our holidays are festive. Our food always tastes like whoever made it loves you. My island says *hello* and you feel seen. My island wants you to snap, expects you to laugh along, is already crying by the time you do.

Here, vulnerability walks freely, buys from mom-and-pop shops. Here, acceptance already has breakfast made by the time you wake up, asks *how'd you sleep?* and actually means it. I was sad on my island once, something about fear and being forgotten, but my island told me, *anyone that comes here chooses it, and anyone that wants to leave can, but if they come, let's give them a reason to stay.* My island is sweet like that.

WHEN I LOST MY FIRST TAEKWONDO TOURNAMENT AT 17 YEARS OLD

my father took my bruised ego and made it go another round
replayed the video of my defeat over and over
forcing me to point out my own flaws
it hurt but I learned humility and how not to lose like that again

my whole life my father's been teaching me how to fight
which two knuckles to hit with for a punch
all punches come from the core
legs are naturally stronger than arms
and knowing how to kick is a must
he critiqued my roundhouse, front, and side kick
my childhood evenings were spent defending:
high, low, middle blocks
he made sure I knew how to defend myself from all sides

my father never talks about what he had to do to get my mother back
my 10 year old self can still feel the vibrations of the fight they had
it shook the mountains we lived on
and now my house shakes with laughter
the two of them smiling
as if they didn't make the other bleed

and I wish my father had taught me instead:
how to come back from the only fight that matters
how to be clutched in the jaws of defeat
and still kiss that mouth afterwards
because I'm replaying in my head the video of my lover
and I'm fighting over and over
and picking out the flaws is not making it better
I still don't know how to defend myself when she throws things
that I cannot block with my hands
or counterattack with a kick

what use is it knowing how to defend myself from all sides
when the arguments we have are pretty straightforward
I have not been trained for this

I've only been taught how to put my foot
on someone's throat if there is no way out
how to disarm and throw to the ground
if my life is in danger
but he never taught me how to hold someone after I've pushed them away
how to start a conversation after we've become fluent in silence
what do I do with my knuckles?
do my feet move towards her or do I slide away?
should I only apologize if it comes from the core?
does my bruised ego sit in silence or do I make it go another round?
at what point is this no longer a fight
and more an opportunity for us to grow?

when I lost my first taekwondo tournament at 17 years old
my father took me under his arm
told me the same Bruce Lee quote he's been saying his whole life

it's like a finger pointing away to the moon
don't concentrate on the finger or you'll miss all that heavenly glory

MY FATHER'S HEART IS LESS LIKE A BLOODY KNUCKLE AFTER A BAR FIGHT AND MORE LIKE THE STITCHES USED TO HEAL THE WOUND

I have never seen my father bleed
but I've seen his scars
proof that he has been opened
proof that time will heal
but remind you of where you came from

my father trained in martial arts since before I was born
if my memory serves
there is a picture of a newborn baby me in my father's black belt uniform
proof that my father wanted me to continue fighting

if my memory serves
when my father was nine
his dad lost his fight with Alzheimer's
then three of my dad's sisters
then his brother
then two more of his sisters
proof that some fights you can't win
some scars you can't see

my heart is less like the punch that breaks the board
and more like the scream that happens during it
the first time I asked my lover if she had seen a certain movie
and she said
yes I saw it with you
I laughed although I wasn't joking
proof that humor is a good defense against scarring
proof that some fights are inherited

last night
I had to remind my father three times
that my dog and my cousin share the same name
and we laughed after each one
proof that laughter can hurt as much as a punch
proof that humor and tears can come from the same place

me and my father's hearts
are less like the picture of us holding each other
when I finally became a black belt
and more like the promise I made him

I will never forget this moment Pa
I will never stop fighting

far, far away

I want to hold all the memories my father is forgetting
want to paint a picture with words the way he did
and insert myself minuscule enough in the moment
to bear witness to my father young and remembering

he used to tell the story of the first time he saw Star Wars
said he saw it opening night May 25th, 1977
then two more times over the weekend
said he didn't have the money to see it again and again
so he and a friend snuck in to see a story set in the stars

my father's story is set in the memories he is forgetting
and the mountains he grew up in
if you were to step into his childhood home
you'd see those memories scatter when the lights turned on

he used to say he saw the lightspeed lines scattering across his eyes
whenever he'd close them
said this movie
of metal birds and star dust
took him out of his world of hungry cows and dirt roads
and placed him in a world of destiny
of second chances
of never knowing your father but still being a good man

my father doesn't remember his father
his father died of Alzheimer's when my father was 9
my father now has Alzheimer's himself
and doesnt remember that he soon will be a grandfather

and I wonder
if part of being a father is forgetting who you were before
or if who you were before reveals himself after you fight with your child

I don't remember the first time I saw star wars
but I do remember when I put it on this past weekend
when it was just my father and me
and he asked me 27 times if this was the last one

na pa, esta es la primera

and each time he would respond with a smile
as if he had a story to tell

MY FATHER IS A COUNTRY BOY I AM A CITY KID

growing up he fell asleep to the coquís' lullaby
me, to the crying of ambulances

he was raised with Spanish sprouting from his tongue
and I had English and Spanish mixing in my soiled mouth

and I couldn't tell which language
was a flower or a weed

when he goes back home, he goes for a run
to see if the people he knows will still be in the places he grew up

when I come home, I sit in my favorite coffee shop
and let the people I think might still be there say hi, if they remember me

we are similar in loving where we come from
but when my father smiles, you are welcomed into family

and I am still learning how to look people in the eye
when I shake their hand

TRUTH IS

the truth is I spent my 20s hurting
myself but mainly
other people because I hurt myself
because I was up to my elbows in concrete
trying to construct a version of myself that could be praiseworthy
someone you could point to and say

that
I want to be like that

but the truth is
I spent my 20s trying to be a good man
but didn't look at who my admiration pointed to
didn't ask myself what being *good* meant
what being a *man* meant
all the men I pointed to had their murals painted on walls

but I didn't want my mural painted on walls
so I turned them into stories instead
repainted my past to make me the hero
or the victim
either way I was still the star
either way these stories were still on walls
either way a collection of walls
      regardless of how pretty they are
      can still form a maze
either way I still ended up becoming half beast
becoming the myth I was trying to avoid
don't praise me now for the monster's head that I hold
because it was mine
these walls were painted with blood

I learned from men who never decentralized themselves
the truth is I never decentralized myself
never thought about the women in my life
that had to carry the weight of my learning curve
never thought about how much the story shifts
when you change perspectives

the truth is most of the men I looked up to were trendsetters
geniuses in their respected fields
pioneers for following their dreams
but never once did they talk about the women they had to leave behind
the families that suffered in the search of their greatness
how a whole generation of boys grew up
hoping to be as hard as the rolling stones they chased after

the truth is I spent my 20s being my father's son
accepted my actions as part of my inheritance
viewed these bodies as a steps to grow
didn't consider
what that growth looked like
until I stopped to notice that my entire forest was on fire
how all this time spent sculpting who I wanted to be left my hands
calloused with the pain I've caused

the truth is now I use my hands for gardening
gotten really good at pulling weeds
gotten really good at watering
at finding the sun's warmth
like the light
at the end of a labyrinth

SIDE EYE WHILE I UBER DRIVE VOLUME 3

so
I refuse to pay $10 a month for SoundCloud Go
meaning I subject myself to commercials
meaning I've grown to hate the Staples guy
meaning I feel hate at least 20 times a day
meaning once again I am choosing pain as a distraction from pain
because I hate driving
because my whole life I've made a living by actually connecting to people
and now
the majority of my passengers just want to drive in silence
which is their right and totally cool
I mean I chose this playlist on purpose
but I also choose not to pay $10 a month for SoundCloud Go
which means I'm choosing to feel enraged
every time a commercial comes on

and this is so me
my mother asked why I'm eating a pizza
when I know I'm lactose intolerant
and I tell her 2 things

1) I do what I want
2) I walk around with an indescribable pain
    a pit of despair and no one knows who dug the hole
    so most days I choose the shovel myself

whether it's dairy
or this job
or the fucking Staples commercial
because the only time I have a break
from this shadow that follows me
is when

is when...

SIDE EYE WHILE I UBER DRIVE VOLUME 4

so
I demand a refund
love isn't the way Ja Rule and Ashanti said it would be
according to them
love could be understood in a 3 minute song
like they warned me that *Pain is Love*
but at least they gave me a catchy hook
like I swear I knew all the words
like I swear all my high school relationships ended
with my shirt off and yelling *it's murda!*

and I wonder
if my passengers in this UberPool grew up with the same soundtrack
because it's 1:30 in the morning
it's been less than 3 minutes since I've picked up the second passenger
and I swear
despite having just met
they've already said I love you to each other
like for real
they asked if I could officiate their wedding
like on dogs
they haven't recited their names yet they've already recited their vows

ya'll
I am 29 and I've said I love you as much as I've said I'm sorry
I'm realizing
my foundation for love rested in the words of a grown man
that wrote the same song for 5 years
like Ashanti made a whole career singing
Although my heart can't take no more I keep on running back to you

and I believed them
believed that love was exactly like it was in the songs
I heard in high school

until I grew up
and realized all the songs still sound like they did in high school
and I wonder where's the growth
and I wonder if I'm talking about the industry
or if I'm talking about myself
and I wonder if I treat relationships the way I do
because I've bought into the loop of romance
of fantasy
of only listening to the songs that talk about the chase
that end with silhouettes and sunsets
or maybe I'm addicted to the heartbreak
the songs that say the things I wish I did
but been told I can't
so I belt them until my voice sounds
like a heart stitching itself back together
I belt them when I'm alone
in my room
in the shower
in my car

and in my car
I am bearing witness to this one hit wonder
finally we approach one of the passenger's destination
and as she prepares to leave
I half expect the guy to ask for her number
for permission to see her
to say some shit like

Come on and get a piece of this late night lover
You know
The one who swing dick like no other
I know

but nothing
she leaves
he is unphased
I turn up the music
and we both sing along
to Drake

FIRST TIME

the first time Anthony saw his father cry he was ten
his mother was unconscious in his father's arms
cradled with the same precision you cradle a newborn
the head resting in the wrinkle of the elbow
the ears positioned symmetrically between the bicep and forearm
  as if to whisper
one day, you will grow out of my safety,
  but I will always attempt to protect you
this was also the first time he saw his father be gentle

the first time Anthony pretended to marry two of his friends was at recess
in second grade
his closest friend at the time wanted to kiss Ashley
the prettiest girl in class
so a plan was devised in which to make this possible
with Anthony playing the role of priest the wedding was set
and as the words
does anyone have a reason as to why these two should not marry
left his lips, the words
Ashley, I want to marry you for more than just a kiss
were trapped behind his teeth
this was also the first time Anthony
pretended that heartbreak was not painful

the first time he ever heard hip-hop
was also the first time he heard his own voice
the first time he performed he got booed off stage
  but it was also the first time he ever felt at home

the first time he witnessed glass shatter
was in the midst of an argument
the exclamation of smash is always louder when done on purpose
this was also the first time he witnessed his father be sorry

the first time Anthony was called monster
he sat in silence as the love he once shared
  hardened into questions he did not have answers to
this was also the first time he was ever named
unlovable

the first time Anthony tasted his own blood he was seven
he and his family were at a park
  and when it was time to return,
Anthony perched at the top of the hill
  he smiled at the only obstacle between him and home
mounted his bike
  and rode down that hill at speeds never before reached
then crashed into a chain-link fence
his face battered and bruised
  leaving a trail of evidence all the way back to the house
but this was also the first time he tasted freedom

the first time Anthony felt safe saying I love you
was after three years of glass shattering
three years of pretending that heartbreak was not painful
there is always a trail of evidence leading to a bruised past
that will prevent you from achieving speeds never before reached
they will taste like words swallowed
they will fit in the wrinkle of your elbow
they will sound like boos but don't let that feel like home
remember the first time you heard your own voice
how it sounded like music
how seeing someone be gentle is their attempt to protect you
how crying may not provide answers but will taste like freedom
even if the prettiest girl in class does not kiss you
you are still loveable

so the next time someone calls you a monster
just smile
and show them the blood in your mouth

I WONDER WHAT RICKY MARTIN IS DOING RIGHT NOW

I wonder
if he has ever used his belly button
  as a hot tub for Gummy Bears
I wonder
what he remembers of his 1999 MTV performance
  of *She's All I Ever Had*

because what I remember
is being with my family at my grandmother's house
huddled in a one-couch living room
surrounding her new TV that her children bought her
as if we were in the front row of his concert
as if watching Ricky Martin perform on MTV meant
we all made it
meant people know Puerto Ricans are here now

but then he appeared on stage
and my man wasn't wearing any shoes
and all I could hear was my aunt behind me asking him why, like

aye Ricky
don't you know that's how they see us mijo?
unworthy of the most basic protection
pero Ricky
esto no es un beach
this was supposed to be the moment
  estos gringos would look up to us
not down at your bare feet

but then
he sang
and with a voice like that he had to be Godly
like he could walk on the waves that brought him here
like no matter what language you spoke at home
he was giving us a voice and the rest of America was singing along

see Ricky knew that this vida would be loca
so he put it into his own mouth
  before the rest of the world could swallow us
he knew
if he could create music to make people move, then maybe
the parents of the girl I crushed on
would ask me to teach them how to dance

instead of asking me to teach them how to say
you're not welcome here in Spanish

see we all knew Ricky Martin wouldn't last
not because his songs could make us feel
but because that's what happens when you are Latino in American media
we are just a fever
just a tickle in the back of your throat you use to call out of work
just a sacrifice to fill your diversity quota

I know what it means now when I hear Spanish in a song
it means

we recognize you exist
but only in the parameters of this chorus

but when I think back to watching him perform on MTV
to seeing someone that looks like me
that came from the same place my parents did
it made me feel like...
I said it made me feel like...

you know when you're young
and you haven't decided
whether or not you believe in God
but you still make wishes when you blow out birthday candles?

yeah
seeing him felt like that

POEM IN THE VOICE OF THE CAT I STAYED WITH FOR 10 DAYS

day one:
meow

I don't know who you are
but you are not the person that loves me
there's a particular way I do things
your presence changes nothing

day two:
oh?
you're still here
I would have thought you'd have left by now
people are constantly walking through these corridors
I pay them no mind
you're no exception

day three:
YOU!
sleeping in the bed that is not yours

feed me

do not think this interaction grants you permission to touch me
we all have to eat

day four:
I have assessed that you are no danger
although you sit on my throne,
I shall allow it
no blood shall be spilled on account of your ignorance
just continue to meet my demands and you may stay
I might even consider letting you caress my fur

day five:
well this is an outrage!
I've never been so insulted in any of my lives
I threw myself down at your feet
extended an invitation for you to hold me
and you brush me off to the side like I am some sort of dog
some alley cat
some stray off the street
don't you know I am the decision-maker here
nothing changes if it does not suit me
and you...

well let's just say I've shared my disappointment
with spots across the house

day six:
fine
you are forgiven
I must say your patience does astound me
despite our debacle the night prior
you released a slight chuckle
cleaned up my mess and began reading again
even apologized for not being more attentive
I have not seen this side of you before

I like it

I am sleeping on the bed tonight
accept it
for it is a fact

day seven:
and to think
I've plotted 10 different ways in which to eliminate you
but your hand on my back feels nice
now my ears, human
scratch behind my ears

day eight:
you are not the person I love
but I found a spot on your chest that is warm
that is welcome home after being gone the whole day
when you sleep
I moonlight over you
touching my whiskers next to yours
well I have to make sure you are breathing
if not who else will get my food?

day nine:
you are not the person I love
but you are water bowl reflection
you are paw print similar
you care about me more than these fans that come to adore me whenever
the doors are open
your intentions are pure
I thank you

day ten:
I woke up
and you were not here
had I known that your hand on my stomach last night
were to be our last moments together
I would have clawed at your wrist
made it more of a challenge
as everything worth loving should be

LOBO DOMESTICADO

the Febos have had a farm in Puerto Rico for three generations
at least
I don't know much of my grandfather
he forgot to document what his childhood
was like before he forgot how to breathe
when Alzheimer's finally took him
my pops
9 yrs old when his father died
doesn't remember what his father was like
he only remembers the way his brothers taught him
what being a man was by taking care of the farm
feed the pigs
move the cows to graze
collect the chicken eggs

his mother tried her best
but raising twelve kids in a home by yourself can feel like a farmhouse

I don't know who in my family initiated the first trade
    my cut of our land for this
    my cut of our land for that
all I know is that whenever we return to his home
my father points to someone else's house and still calls it ours
points to land consumed with other people's dreams
and still calls it a nightmare

I wonder when my family first started to show their teeth
snarling at what they didn't have
while the things that they did started to suffer

a family of farmers turned into werewolves at the sight of a promise

my family fed on the very breath that gave us life
turned us into animals before our animals' eyes
an unchecked hunger for anything whole
turned into chunks of our lands sold to men
with silver in their teeth
who traveled in packs with torches leading the way
I wonder if this is why the men in my family can act like monsters
and still call that tradition

when I first learned that the light of the moon
reflected off a pretty girl's smile
could elongate my jaw
make me howl like my mother didn't teach me how to use my tongue
it was already too late
trust dripping from my hairy chin
I love you's crushed by the weight of my paws
I never intended to be such a beast
I just learned how to be a man from a man who was raised by men
that killed what they took care of

now my cousin takes care of the house that was supposed to be mine
because my father
with his huffing and puffing on someone else's doorstep
blew what we had away;
at my uncle's home down the road
my cousin built an area for a pig roast
on the side of the house made out of bricks

but this will not be me
this will not be my legacy
not again
not after the animal led me to a pile of bodies at my doorstep
holes where their hearts should be
and my hands were heavy
with bone fragments caught under my fingernails

MEN IN MY FAMILY

my 12-year-old cousin is now a year older
than I was when I lived in Puerto Rico
he is who I could have been if we never moved
he sleeps in what was my sister's room in the house my dad
and his brothers built for us to grow old in
and the room that was mine is now a time capsule
to all the memories built up until we left
and my old toy chest is there
and baby pictures that once laid claim to these walls
are now home to lagartijos that have withered and died

and I think I understand irony better now
or at least what happens when you try to hold memories
and still end up forgetting

and last night I reminisced with cousins that would not have recognized
me if they saw me on the street
and we all laughed at who we've become
and they tell me about the friends we had when I lived here
and they all have kids
and some of them are in jail
and some of them are dead
and I love how much has changed
and I love how much has stayed the same

and I think I understand paradoxes better now
or at least what happens when your childhood loves you back

and despite the short time I lived here
walking through the farm still feels like home
and despite the even shorter time I lived in this house walking through
the halls still feels like a battlefield
   I still hear the shattering glass
   I still see my mother's hungry knife

I still see her hungrier teeth
I still smell my father's blood
I still feel my sister's trembling body
I've never felt more like a big brother than that night
I don't think I've been a good brother since
I think about what my father has learned from his brothers
I think about what I have learned from my father

and my fiancée asked me about the men in my family
and I tell her

around these parts
Febo is synonymous with infidelity

I think I understand *legacy* better now
or at least what happens when you let a ghost define you

and I hope this house isn't haunted
and I hope the men in my family don't chalk this up to a curse
and I fear for my 12-year-old cousin
and the lovers he might hold
and the lovers he might break
and I fear the day he comes home with a heart in his hand
and no one will ask whose it is
and the men in my family will tell him to feed it to the pigs

like they were taught
by the men before them

6/17/18

and when the earth calls me home
and dictates I stop growing

may I never stop growing

bury me next to a tree
no casket
no tombstone
just my body continuing to do what it always has:
giving itself to anything that helps people breathe
connecting me to whatever has roots that long to go deeper

bury me here
and watch as the tree redefines what is expected of it:
this summer each of my branches hold a mango
and the next summer an orange

winter, I let go of my leaves
but I have hollowed my trunk
to provide space for those who seek refuge

this is where I find peace in death:
the knowledge that just because my body is gone
it doesn't mean that what I tried to nourish is too

SHADOWS

I stopped going by Anthony around the same time I started to grow
resentment toward my father
all his too much was too much
his constant arm around people
his constant retelling of the same stories
even his sneezes demand attention

Anthony is the English version of Antonio
and although my dad prefers Tony
it was too close
and any association with him
was an island I wanted to leave

I started going by Febo around the same time I wanted
pride in something
I've heard stories of our name
how anyone with it was family
how we came from nothing
got a little more
and used our name to build a reputation

we worked with our hands
were faithful tending our lands and our God
were faithful talking shit and drinking
faithful to being the first and last at the party
but not to women

now I am not proud of that
not proud of how my many cousins share our fathers'
last name but not a relationship with them

not proud that my father followed in his brothers' footsteps
and it led him to a bed that wasn't his
not proud that in the attempt to reclaim my name
I made my family's name proud by living up to it
that my disdain for my father caused me to act like him

is a wraith the correct name for a shadow that's been around so long
you feel like you were born into it?

when my father found out why I was living in the basement
why my mother stopped talking to me
he came down and told me he wasn't proud
and it's only now I can see how scared he was
to be Frankenstein to this monster
to see Mr. Hyde outside his body
to talk to me about the shadows that come with being a Febo
and I can't believe I didn't see his growth until now

Is there a name for that?

not long ago
my wife and I went with my parents and my sister
to my dad's neurological appointment
his early onset Alzheimer's doesn't feel as early anymore
the doctor went down the list of my father's 11 siblings
reading each name out loud
my mother confirming the cause of death for the dead
the current condition of the living

out of his eleven
one died of breast cancer
seven of Alzheimer's
and the four that remain
all have it

I know any children we have
will have no memories with my dad
I know any children we have
will inherit the light of our name
and with luck not its shadow

and I know
if blessed with the opportunity
we will name our first boy
Antonio.

GOOD MORNING

good morning heartbreak
you have filled these balloon lungs with a helium
that has made pronouncing her name
a pitch higher with every breath
I cannot sleep now
since I keep her presence in my mouth with every prayer
I've become so high
I speak to God directly

good morning regret
like my breath
you remind me of yesterday by leaving a foul taste in my mouth
lies lodged in my molars
only accessible with my tongue
I say them as often as apologies

good morning self pity
you are never where I want to be
but always the place I find myself
you are a direct result of her absence
your darkness comes with the fleeing of light
footsteps on the moon only a few have ever seen
the silence between lightning
and thunder
you are a reminder that she is not here
you have replaced the life on my sleeves with frost
make me question if I want to live in New England
you linger
like she did the last time I saw her
smiling, as if nothing was wrong

good morning loneliness
you are louder in bed than I imagined

I thought you'd would have left by now
I guess
I'll go make us some coffee

good morning envy
I've called you inspiration for the last three years
a wolf in sheep's clothing
the sugar in a cupcake
the tears in my hello
I never wanted to wake up next to you
but you found your way under my pillow
  the same day she proved she could live without me
there is nothing more excruciating than her success
how she is where I could be if I just let her go
how my finish line
is just a few feet in front of me
but feels as removed as she's become
my pride
is lost in between the changing of the time zones
her new area code
is the daily number of thoughts she does not think of me
while I
have thought of nine hundred and seventy eight different reasons
  why we should be together when really
there are more reasons why we shouldn't

good morning revelation
I did not hear you come in
last time I saw you
you looked so small in the distance I thought you were leaving
well I'm so glad you can join us

good morning healing
thank you
for the breakfast in bed
the sliding of the curtains
the opening of the window
I know you didn't make the birds sing
but thank you for making me listen
for the sun on my skin
for reminding me
that I too could be warm

I guess
it is a good morning after all

Acknowledgements

First and foremost shoutout to you for reading this. For taking the time to engage with me in this body of work. However you feel about it, I hope something resonated with you and that you push it forward.

I want to give a shout out to my family. To you mami, Madeline Febo, la rena, la gata, te amo bella. To you papi, Antonio Febo, Master Febo, sigue dando centellasos, nuca te olvidare. To you sis, Karina Febo, we are figuring this thing out together, we are learning how to love each other and, God willing, we have so much time to practice. To my wife, Carlie Febo, #sayyesandcry, I love you mama. To our daughter Luna Febo, this is an artifact of my life before I met you, and I'm so thankful to have met you. To our pets, our large orange cat Finn, our locita Frenchie Coco, and RIP to the realist one, our first Frenchie, Oscar. Y'all make it a home.

To my honorary big bro and sis, Willie and Jomari, you know I love y'all. Thank you for showing me the way. To all my Santiago's, los amo y gracias por quiéreme. To all the Febos, ¡Febo en la casa puñ**!*

To all the main homies, my heart and time and presence is always available for you: Joey Banh, Masada Jones, JuanCarlos Rivera, Amanda Torres, Ella Quimby.

To my partner in thyme, and the other half of Adobo-Fish-Sauce, Ricky Orng. Our continued collaboration and friendship has meant the world to me.

To my community of poets and artists, thank you for your inspiration and the amazing work you do that makes me want to step up to the plate. Y'all, our contemporaries are dope: Will Giles, Porsha Olayiwola, Oompa, Janae Johnson, Jonathan Mendoza, Cliff Notez, Hipstory, Mason Granger, Muggs Fogarty, Justice Ameer Gaines, Zenaida Peterson, Princess Moon, Katytarika Bartel, Sarah Masse, Emmanuel Oppong-Yeboah, Victoria Delvalle, Dubem Oak, Sydney Bobb, Carolyn Parker-Fairbain, Lissa Piercy, Alex Charalambides, Harlym 1Two5, Jason Henry Simon-Bierenbaum, Clint Smith, Eve Ewing, Lauren Whitehead.

Shout out to the Game Over Books squad for giving these poems a home. And a special shout out to Josh Savory and Kaleigh O'Keefe for keeping the dream alive.

And I wouldn't be here if not for the spaces and orgs that have shaped me: FreeVerse!, Untitled Open Mic, House Slam, Cantab, FEMS, UTEC, MassLeap, Institute of Contemporary Art Boston.

Last but not least—shout out to Lowell, Massachusetts and Canóvanas, Puerto Rico. Y'all in my bones.

Biography

Anthony Febo is a Puerto Rican poet, artist, and new dad living in Cambridge, Massachusetts. Febo has been performing and teaching poetry and theatre for over a decade. In the classroom, Febo treats each workshop as its own celebration. He teaches through his own process for creation and self reflection called Slinging—rooted in mindfulness, habit and routines, and Visual Thinking Strategies. It draws on his experiences in theatre spaces, museums, non-profits, and art centers. On the stage, he has toured the country individually and as half of Adobo-Fish-Sauce, a cooking and poetry collaboration. His work examines what it means to actively choose joy in the face of what is trying to break you. Weaving performance into his writing, he examines issues such as toxic masculinity, family, culture, identity, and the role representation plays in a person's development.